Everyday Korean

First Phrases from Around the World

Tricia Hoffman

Little Mitchie
an imprint of Mitchell Lane

CREATING YOUNG NONFICTION READERS

Little Mitchie books spark curiosity and support early nonfiction reading for students in Grades 2-3. Designed to build vocabulary, support second language learners, and prepare readers for middle-grade content, each book includes helpful tips for parents and educators to build confidence and deepen understanding of the world.

TIPS FOR READING NONFICTION WITH BEGINNING READERS

Talk about Nonfiction

Begin by explaining that nonfiction books give us information that is true. The book will be organized around a specific topic or idea, and we may learn new facts through reading.

Look at the Parts

Most nonfiction books have helpful features. Our *Little Mitchie* titles include color photographs and graphic aids, a table of contents, a glossary, and an index. Share the purpose of these features with your reader.

Color Photos and Graphic Aids

A lot of information can be found by "reading" photos, charts, maps, and other graphic aids found within nonfiction texts. Help your reader learn more about the different ways information can be displayed.

Table of Contents

Located at the front of the book, this list shows the big ideas within the text and the page numbers where they can be found.

Index

Located at the back of the book, an index is an alphabetical list of topics and the page numbers where they can be found.

With a little help and guidance about reading nonfiction, you can feel good about introducing a young reader to the world of *Little Mitchie* nonfiction books.

Little Mitchie is an imprint of:

Mitchell Lane
PUBLISHERS

2001 SW 31st Avenue
Hallandale, FL 33009
mitchelllanepub.com

First Edition, 2027.

Author: Tricia Hoffman
Designer: Kathy Walsh
Editor: Tricia Hoffman

Library of Congress Cataloging-in-Publication Data
Title: Everyday Korean / by Tricia Hoffman

Description: Hallandale, FL :
Mitchell Lane Publishers, [2027]

Identifiers:
Library bound ISBN: 979-8-89260-910-4
Paperback ISBN: 979-8-90145-061-1
eBook ISBN: 979-8-90145-020-8

Library of Congress Control Number: 2026930173

PHOTO CREDITS: Cover and Title pg: iukhym_vova, smile3377; Doodle Art: devitaayu, FourLeafLover, wanchana, veekicl, Rizky, mhatzapa, Kebon doodle, Asyam Design, piixypeach, syoko: istock: background, rica nohara; p 4, Ronnie Chua, miya227, Utoimage; p 5, AnurakPongpatimet; p 6, Q88, Kitreel; p 7, Eric Isselee, Utoimage; p 9, Anurak Pongpatimet; p 10, Golfx, Zhane Luk, MaeManee; p 11, Bangkok Click Studio; p 12, all_about_people, Chiociolla, Chase D'animulls, BongoStock; p 13, Bet_Noire, Monkey Business Images; p 14, wavebreakmedia, 88Stockvn, Four.Stock; p 15, zEdward_Indy, sfaafaa; p 16, metamorworks, Utoimage, Nattawat Arunkasem; p 17, StockLab, p 18, imtmphoto, kornphoto, 88Stockvn; p 19, kornphoto; p 20, metamorowrks, 88Stockvn; p 21, Ann in the uk, gowithstock, Dikey Creative Labs Photo, Anurak Pongpatimet; p22, suriyachan, Pixel-Shot; p 23, Hananeko_Studio

Table of Contents

This Is Me

annyeonghaseyo!

Hello!

jeoneun ahob sal-ibnida.

I am nine years old.

je ileum-eun baeghyeon-ibnida.

My name is Baek-Hyeon.

ige balo naya

hana
one

dul
two

set
three

net
four

daseos
five

yeoseot
six

ilgop
seven

yeodeol
eight

ahop
nine

yeol
ten

annyeonghi gaseyo!

Goodbye!

People and Pets

jeoneun gajoggwa hamkke salgo issseubnida.

I live with my family.

abeoji
father

hyeongje
brother

eomeoni
mother

jamae
sister

salamgwa banlyeodongmul

Today

oneul-eun
suyoil-ibnida.

Today is Wednesday.

il-yoil
Sunday

wol-yoil
Monday

hwayoil
Tuesday

suyoil
Wednesday

mog-yoil
Thursday

geum-yoil
Friday

toyoil
Saturday

jigeum-eun sip-i-worieyo.
The month is December.

il-wol . . . . January
i-wol. . . . . February
sam-wol . . . . . March
sa-wol . . . . April
o-wol . . . . May
yu-wol . . . . June
chil-wol . . . . . . July
pal-wol . . . . . . August
gu-wol. . . . . . . September
sip-wol. . . . . . . October
sip-il-wol . . . . . November
sip-i-wol . . . . . December

oneul

bakk-i chubseubnida.

It is cold outside.

hwachanghan

sunny

deop-da

hot

bioneun

rainy

kkamjjag nollan

windy

Morning

joh-eun achim-ieyo!

Good morning!

naneun meolileul bisneunda.

I comb my hair.

naneun ileul dakkneunda.

I brush my teeth.

achim

jeoneun geomeun saek bajireul ipseubnida.

I wear black pants.

juhwangsaek orange	noransaek yellow	paransaek blue
bunhongsaek pink	borasaek purple	ppalgansaek red
choroksaek green	geomeunsaek black	huinsaek white

Breakfast

toseuteu
toast

achim-eulo silieol juseyo.

I want cereal for breakfast, please.

olenji juseu
orange juice

beikeon
bacon

gyelan
egg

achimsiksa

beoseuga dochaghaess-eoyo. ije chulbalhal sigan-ieyo!

The bus is here. It is time to go!

baenang
backpack

seukulbeoseu
school bus

School

jeoneun haggyoe gabnida.

I go to school.

naneun chaegeul ilkneunda.

I read.

jeoneun suhag-eul habnida.

I do math.

haggyo

doum-i pil-yohaeyo.

I need help.

chaegsang

desk

seonsaengnim

teacher

hwajangsil-e gado doelkkayo?

May I go to the bathroom?

Time to Play

jeorang gachi nollae-yo?

Will you play with me?

ye!

Yes!

naneun dallinda.
I run.

naneun seuwinghanda.
I swing.

nol sigan

naneun gong-eul deonjinda.

I throw a ball.

gwi
ears

ib
mouth

pal
arm

dali
leg

bal
foot

Neighborhood

jeoneun dongnae salgo isseoyo.

I live in a neighborhood.

naneun chinguege son-eul heundeul-eossda.

I wave to my friend.

naneun gagee ganda.

I go to the store.

ius

igeos-eun eolmaingayo?

How much does this cost?

Dinner

jeonyeog sigsa sigan-ingayo?

Is it time for dinner?

ne, butagdeulibnida.
Yes, please.

aniyo, gwaenchanhseubnida.
No, thank you.

jeonyeog

jeoneun hangug eumsig-eul joh-ahaeyo.

I like Korean food.

kimchi
soup

jeoneun migug eumsig-eul joh-ahaeyo.

I like American food.

haembeogeo
hamburger

gamja twigim
french fries

japchae
noodles

Night

jeoneun jam-os-eul ib-eoyo.

I wear pajamas.

jeoneun jamjareo gayo.

I go to bed.

naneun nun-eul gamneunda.

I close my eyes.

bam

dam-yo
blanket

begae
pillow

Index

About Korean

Korean is the 13th most common language in the world. It is spoken by more than 80 million people. Many Korean speakers live in South Korea and North Korea. There are also more than two million Korean speakers in China and one million in the United States. Many live in Japan as well. Korean uses a writing system called Hangul that consists of 24 letters. One unique thing about Korean is that it does not use any capital letters. It also does not use articles like *a* or *the*.